PEOPLES *of* NORTH AMERICA

Seminole

VALERIE BODDEN

CREATIVE PAPERBACKS

· PEOPLES of NORTH AMERICA ·

Seminole

VALERIE BODDEN

CREATIVE EDUCATION · CREATIVE PAPERBACKS

Published by Creative Education and Creative Paperbacks
P.O. Box 227, Mankato, Minnesota 56002
Creative Education and Creative Paperbacks
are imprints of The Creative Company
www.thecreativecompany.us

Design and production by Christine Vanderbeek
Art direction by Rita Marshall
Printed in China

Photographs by Alamy (AAA Photostock, Pat Canova, Michele and Tom Grimm, North Wind
Picture Archives, M. Timothy O'Keefe, RosaIreneBetancourt 6, Science History Images, State
Archives of Florida/Florida Memory, ZUMA Press, Inc.), Corbis (Scott Leslie/Minden Pictures,
Phil Schermeister), Creative Commons Wikimedia (George Catlin, Ralph Eleaser Whiteside Earl/
Executive Office of the President of the United States, National Park Service, U.S. Marine Corps/
U.S. National Archives and Records Administration, U.S. National Archives and Records
Administration), Getty Images (Archive Photos/Stringer, Bettmann, George Rinhart, Marilyn
Angel Wynn), iStockphoto (Juanmonino), Shutterstock (fivespots, iofoto, SMIRNOVA IRINA,
OHishiapply, Transia Design), Smithsonian Institution (Department of Anthropology,
Smithsonian Institution/National Museum of the American Indian), SuperStock (Everett
Collection, Illustrated London News Ltd/Mar/Pantheon)

Library of Congress Cataloging-in-Publication Data
Names: Bodden, Valerie, author.
Title: Seminole / Valerie Bodden.
Series: Peoples of North America.
Includes bibliographical references and index.
Summary: A history of the people and events that influenced the North American Indian tribe
known as the Seminole, including warrior Osceola and conflicts such as the Seminole Wars.
Identifiers: LCCN 2017044008 / ISBN 978-1-60818-967-0 (hardcover) /
ISBN 978-1-62832-594-2 (pbk) / ISBN 978-1-64000-068-1 (eBook)
Subjects: LCSH: Seminole Indians—History—Juvenile literature.
Classification: LCC E99.S28 B64 2018 / DDC 975.9004/973859—dc23

CCSS: RI.5.1, 2, 3, 5, 6, 8, 9; RH.6-8.4, 5, 6, 7, 8, 9

First Edition HC 9 8 7 6 5 4 3 2 1
First Edition PBK 9 8 7 6 5 4 3 2 1

PEOPLES *of* NORTH AMERICA

Seminole

VALERIE BODDEN

CREATIVE EDUCATION • CREATIVE PAPERBACKS

Table of Contents

⊰─ SEMINOLE COUPLE IN TRADITIONAL CLOTHING (ON
PAGE 3); CHICKEE HUTS IN FLORIDA'S EVERGLADES
(PICTURED HERE). ─⊱

Introduction

The people known as the Seminole Indians once floated silently in canoes through the thick swamps of the Everglades in present-day Florida. This hot, humid landscape teemed with life. Grasses taller than a person's head grew from the shallow water that covered much of the land. The swamp's scattered high points, known as hammocks, supported dense clusters of cypress, willow, oak, and wax myrtle trees. Alligators, snakes, turtles, and fish filled the waters. Deer and panthers roamed the hammocks. More than 350 species of birds, including egrets, herons, and terns, made their home in the wetland. The Seminole found everything they needed for food and shelter in these swamps. Most importantly, they found thick cover that allowed them to disappear from pursuing American soldiers.

The name "Seminole" may have come from a Creek Indian word meaning "runaway." This might refer to the Seminole's breaking away from the Creek in the 1700s. Or, the word may come from the Spanish word *cimarrón*, meaning "wild." Although the Seminole at first enjoyed a relatively isolated life in Florida, it didn't last long. As Americans grew hungry for land in the 1800s, soldiers pursued the Seminole into the swamps. The Seminole launched a fierce defense and held out through three wars. Although many Seminole were eventually forced to leave their land to resettle in Indian Territory (present-day Oklahoma), others resisted. They remained in Florida, where today they continue to cling to their traditional culture while also adapting to the modern world.

ALLIGATORS IN THE EVERGLADES FREQUENT LARGE, CIRCULAR-SHAPED PATCHES OF CYPRESS TREES, CALLED CYPRESS DOMES.

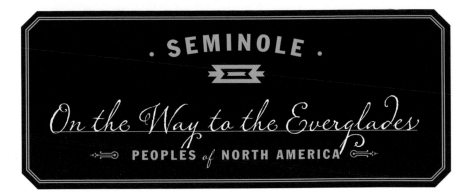

. SEMINOLE .

On the Way to the Everglades

PEOPLES *of* NORTH AMERICA

lthough the Seminole eventually settled in Florida, **ANTHROPOLO-GISTS** do not believe they were the original inhabitants of this region. Instead, between 100,000 and 200,000 Indians belonging to 50 or more other nations likely inhabited the Florida of the early 1500s. Many of these native groups may have lived on the peninsula for thousands of years. Among them were the Calusa, who hunted and fished in the southern part of the peninsula. The Apalachee farmed in western Florida, while the Timucua settled in the north.

When Spanish explorers arrived in 1513, they brought new diseases such as smallpox and measles. The Indians had never been exposed to these diseases before, and their immune systems were unable to fight them off. By the 1600s, thousands of Florida's Indians had died of disease. Others were killed in wars with Spanish settlers or were taken captive by British slave traders. By the early 1700s, almost no **INDIGENOUS** peoples remained in Florida.

Meanwhile, to the north, the Creek people dominated present-day Alabama and Georgia. The Creek lived in more than 60 towns scattered along the region's rivers and creeks (the source of their name). These towns were separated into two divisions. The Upper Creek spoke the Muskogee language.

THE FIRST RECORDED LANDING IN FLORIDA OC-CURRED MORE THAN 20 YEARS AFTER COLUMBUS REACHED THE NEW WORLD.

TRADE BROUGHT COLONISTS AND AMERICAN INDIANS TOGETHER, BUT LAND CLAIMS CAUSED TROUBLE.

They were sometimes called the Red Sticks for their habit of marking off the days until the start of a war using red sticks which were delivered to the enemy. The Lower Creek spoke the Mikasuki (also known as Hitchiti) language.

In the early 1700s, some Lower Creek bands began to migrate from Georgia into Florida. One reason may be that they feared retaliation from British settlers after some Creek towns joined in a war against the British. Some may also have been discontent with the growing power of the Creek **CONFEDERACY** over their towns. Others may have moved to be closer to Florida's abundant game. Or they may have been searching for fertile land where they could farm without worrying about enemies such as the Cherokee, Choctaw, and Chickasaw nearby.

The Creek migration lasted more than 100 years. During this time, small bands and family groups made their way south from British-controlled Georgia into Spanish-owned Florida. They established permanent settlements in the northern part of the peninsula. In some cases, they joined the few remaining indigenous peoples already in the region.

Initially, most Creeks who migrated to Florida still considered themselves part of the Creek Confederacy. But over time, the Indians in Florida began to see themselves as a separate people. By the 1780s or '90s, they seem to have cut off almost all ties with the Creek. They were now Seminole.

Throughout the late 1700s and early 1800s, the Seminole population continued to grow. Members of several other southeastern tribes, including the Shawnee and Yuchi, also sought refuge in Florida. These refugees became part of the Seminole people. After the Creek War of 1814, in which the Creek were defeated by the United States Army, several Upper Creek moved into Florida and

Being Seminole

⟶≈⟵ **OSCEOLA** ⟶≈⟵ *Born in 1804 in an Upper Creek town in Alabama,* **OSCEOLA** *moved with his mother's band to Florida as a boy. He fought in the First Seminole War before rising to a leadership position during the Second Seminole War after killing a pro-removal Seminole leader. American newspapers followed the exploits of the flamboyantly dressed Osceola throughout the second war. Many Americans rooted for his success and protested his capture under a white flag. His death in 1838 was mourned across the country.*

SEMINOLE CHIEF
CO-EE-HÁ-JO
(PICTURED) WAS
IMPRISONED
WITH OSCEOLA
IN 1837.

joined the Seminole as well. Because they were made up of both Upper and Lower Creek, some Seminole bands spoke Muskogee, while others spoke Mikasuki. The two languages were not mutually intelligible; speakers of one could not necessarily understand the other.

The Seminole maintained traditional Creek clan divisions in Florida. Clans consisted of related family groups. The Seminole traced a person's descent on the female side. Children belonged to the clan of their mothers. Traditional Seminole clans included Panther, Otter, Wildcat, Bird, and Wolf. The members of a clan were believed to share characteristics with the animal and namesake of their clan. Panther clan members were considered quiet, for example. Because they were related, members of the same clan could not marry. If the last female member of a clan died, the Seminole said that the clan's "fire was put out."

As they settled into life in northern Florida, the Seminole continued to build Creek-style homes made of logs. They plastered the logs with a mixture of mud and straw. Cypress-bark shingles formed the roof. Many homes were made of two to four separate small buildings. Others were two stories tall and might have a porch.

⊸═ CRIME AND PUNISHMENT ═⊶ *Those who broke tribal rules often faced punishments. If the crime was not serious, the accused might be excluded from the ceremonial life of the tribe until he or she was willing to change. For more serious crimes, however, a person might be whipped, beaten, or fined. Sometimes, a person's hair, ears, or nose might be cropped, or cut. The worst offenders were executed. Such punishments were often determined on Court Day of the Green Corn Dance and carried out by the town's war leaders.*

At first, the Seminole arranged their homes into Creek-style towns. Each settlement likely consisted of 8 to 30 homes arranged around a central square. Each home had a small garden patch, where the family planted corn, beans, and squash. In addition, everyone was expected to work in the community corn and tobacco fields outside the town. When the soil became infertile, the entire town was moved. The surrounding land was used for hunting as well. In some settlements, people also herded cattle that had been abandoned by the Spanish and earlier Indian groups.

The Seminole remained in northern Florida for a time. But by the early to mid-1800s, the arrival of American settlers pushed many to seek refuge in the swamps and wetlands of southern Florida. Faced with a new, marshy landscape, the Seminole completely changed the style of their dwellings. In place of log cabins, they began to construct *chickees*. These open-sided structures consisted of a platform elevated about three feet (0.9 m) above the ground and covered with a **THATCHED** roof. The open sides allowed cooling breezes to circulate, while the thatched roof and elevated platform kept people and belongings dry during rainstorms and floods. In addition, chickees could be built quickly—an important

SEMINOLE SPEAR-FISHED FROM DUGOUT CANOES (ABOVE) AND STAYED DRY UNDER THATCHED CHICKEE ROOFS (RIGHT).

factor when the Seminole were being pursued by the U.S. military.

Chickees were generally erected among the trees of a hammock. Instead of large towns, the Seminole now lived in smaller camps. They grew corn and pumpkins on the hammocks. But they also collected wild nuts, berries, and fruits, as well as the roots of the coontie plant, from which they made flour. They fished and hunted alligators, deer, and other animals.

Life in the swamps required boats. The Seminole built dugout canoes by piling embers from a fire onto a cypress log 12 to 30 feet (3.7–9.1 m) long. Once the embers had burned through, the Indians scraped away the charred wood until the log was hollowed out. Seminole dugouts had flat bottoms and a high, pointed bow, or front. They were maneuvered through shallow water by a man standing on a platform in the back of the boat. He used a long pole to push off the muddy swamp floor.

The Seminole had little contact with other American Indians, since there were few remaining in Florida. However, they traded with British and Spanish settlers. In return for deerskins, alligator hides, and bird feathers, they received guns, iron tools, cloth, beads, and alcohol. Sometimes the Seminole sailed larger canoes to Cuba or the Bahamas to trade as well.

As they traveled through Florida, the Seminole made use of all that the land provided them. They believed their Great Spirit had given them this land, and they had no intention of leaving it.

When they moved to Florida, the earliest Seminole towns maintained a form of government similar to the Creek's. Gradually, some aspects of Creek political organization began to disappear. A Seminole town was led by a *mikko*, or chief. The position of mikko was hereditary, passed down on the mother's side. If the chief died, the next in line for the chieftainship was his younger brother. The youngest brother was followed by the oldest son of the chief's oldest sister. A chieftainship was generally for life, although a mikko could be removed from the position if he failed to perform his duties. A chief's main responsibilities included issuing invitations to feasts and overseeing taxes, which the people paid with a portion of their crops. These payments were used to provide food for poorer members of the town.

The mikko also headed the town council. The council consisted of prominent men who met daily to discuss important topics such as war, hunting, and planting. The council also settled disagreements among members of the town. Councilmen served as advisers to the chief, who retained the authority to make final decisions.

Together, the mikko and the council determined when to make war. Once war had been declared, the war chiefs took over leadership. They

BILLY BOWLEGS III WAS A HISTORIAN WHO TAUGHT AMERICANS ABOUT SEMINOLE TRADITIONS IN THE LATE 1800S AND EARLY 1900S.

prepared supplies, recruited warriors, and directed military operations. All Seminole men were expected to fight when needed. Before going into battle, the men drank water with snakeroot. The war chiefs told them, "Don't be afraid. Something sharp will come. But the powers above will take care of you." The men fought nearly naked, although they painted their bodies red and black, the colors of war.

The warriors moved out in a single-file line behind their leader. The last person in the line carefully covered the group's tracks. Moving silently, the Seminole communicated with hand signals on the trail. A **SHAMAN**, or medicine man, brought along plants to treat injuries.

By the time they settled in Florida, most Seminole had acquired guns. But the warriors had little training in the use of firearms. Their shots often missed their mark. In addition, they often loaded the wrong amount of powder, making the weapons ineffective. Sometimes, so little powder was used that the shell would simply bounce off the enemy's body. The Seminole also carried bows to shoot arrows made of cane stalks with a fire-hardened tip. They carried knives and tomahawks they had obtained in trade as well.

The Seminole usually engaged in **GUERRILLA** attacks. As they launched an attack, they might let out a fierce shriek to frighten the enemy. In general, they preferred not to fight at night. They believed the souls of those killed in the dark would be unable to find their way to peace.

Apart from making war, men were responsible for hunting.

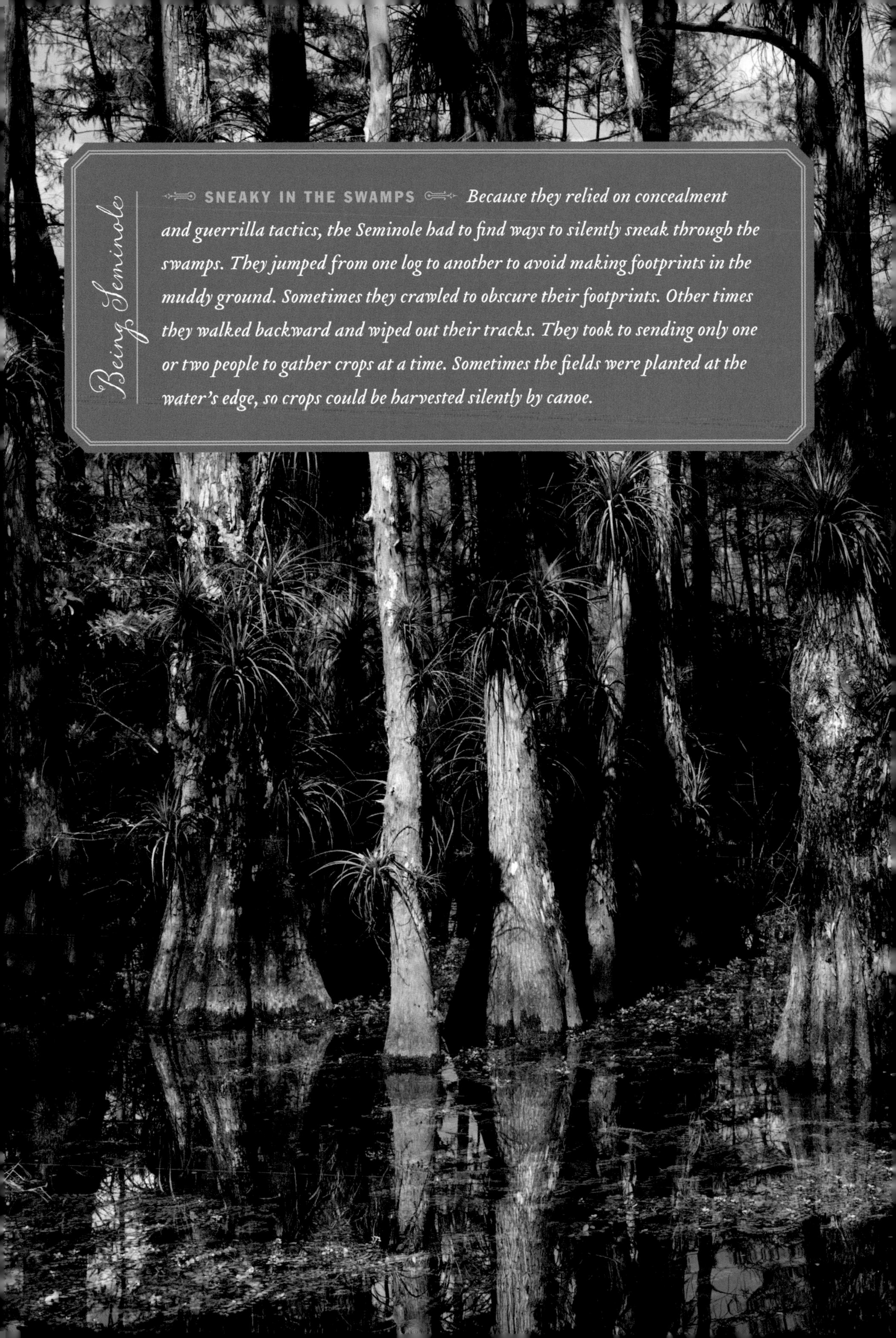

Being Seminole

SNEAKY IN THE SWAMPS *Because they relied on concealment and guerrilla tactics, the Seminole had to find ways to silently sneak through the swamps. They jumped from one log to another to avoid making footprints in the muddy ground. Sometimes they crawled to obscure their footprints. Other times they walked backward and wiped out their tracks. They took to sending only one or two people to gather crops at a time. Sometimes the fields were planted at the water's edge, so crops could be harvested silently by canoe.*

Traveling in groups of two or three, they used guns or bows and arrows to hunt deer. They trapped smaller animals such as rabbits and shot birds with blowguns. In the swamps, they hunted alligators. One technique involved pushing a log down a gator's throat and flipping it over. Then the Seminole speared or clubbed the animal.

Men also took responsibility for burning trees and brush to clear land for planting. They watched the fields at night to keep bears, deer, and raccoons away from the crops. Both men and women worked the fields.

In addition to working the fields, women gathered wild plants, including coontie (for the starchy roots) and wild potatoes. They made pottery and baskets as well as all their family's clothing. Men's clothing included a breechcloth covered by a shirt that fell almost to the knees. Traditionally, men wore no pants. They often wore colorful turbans on their heads. Women wore long skirts with short shirts that stopped above the waist. In the mid-1800s, Seminole women began creating clothing in a new style known as patchwork. Patchwork clothing was made by sewing bright strips of cloth together.

Seminole women also took care of the children. From the age of four, children began to help with simple chores, such as gathering wood or kneading dough. As they grew up, boys began to hunt and fish, while girls learned to cook and sew. Family members sometimes disciplined a misbehaving child by scratching him or her on the leg with a needle.

A young man who wanted to marry a girl had the women of his family inform the girl's family. Afterward, he sent gifts to the girl. If she accepted, they were married, often without a special ceremony. The couple lived with the bride's family for a time before establishing their own home.

PATCHWORK CLOTHING BECAME MORE COMMON AS THE SEMINOLE GAINED ACCESS TO HAND-CRANKED SEWING MACHINES.

SEMINOLE GIRLS
AND WOMEN WORE
DOZENS OF BEADED
NECKLACES, AND
BOYS AND MEN
WORE HATS OR
TURBANS.

As they went about their daily lives, the Seminole were always aware of the spiritual world. They believed that everything, whether living or nonliving, possessed a soul. The Seminole also believed in several gods. The most important were the Creator, also known as the Master of Breath, and the Sun. Other gods included Sacred Fire, Moon, Thunder, Corn, and Four Winds.

A boy considered to have a strong connection with the spirit world might be chosen to serve as shaman. First, he needed several years of training. Seminole shaman Josie Billie told one anthropologist, "In order to cure one must learn the proper magical chants and formulas. Hence the teaching of the songs in connection with each one of the various types of disease undoubtedly forms a significant part of the training of a new medicine man." The shaman was responsible for guarding the medicine bundle, a collection of sacred items that was believed to have great power. In addition, the shaman chanted over the sick, prayed for good weather, and interpreted dreams.

Among the most important duties of the shaman was leading ceremonies. The most significant ceremony was the Green Corn Dance, or Busk. Held each year in July or August to celebrate the ripening corn, this ceremony marked the beginning of a new year. It began with several days of dances and games. Then, on Court Day, the men drank a special tea brewed from the leaves of the yaupon, an evergreen holly. Europeans later dubbed the tea "black drink" because of its color. The Seminole, however, called it white drink because they believed it was sacred. According to American military officer Caleb Swan, who attended a late-1700s Seminole ceremony at which participants drank the tea, "They have a religious belief that it purifies them from all sin, and leaves them in a state of perfect innocence; that it inspires them with an invincible prowess in war; and that it is the only solid cement of friendship, benevolence, and hospitality." On Court Day, trials were held for those accused of committing crimes. In addition, the shaman displayed the medicine bundle on this day. That night, young men received their adult names. The final day of the Green Corn Dance involved a rich feast of newly harvested corn.

LED BY A MEDICINE MAN, SEMINOLE PERFORM THE STOMP DANCE SEVERAL TIMES DURING THE ANNUAL BUSK.

· SEMINOLE ·
From Contact to Conflict
PEOPLES *of* NORTH AMERICA

The Spanish had entered Florida long before the Seminole arrived. In 1513, Juan Ponce de León claimed Florida for the Spanish crown. From 1539 through 1540, Spanish explorer Hernando de Soto traveled through Florida and into Georgia. He was the first European to make contact with the Creek. By the time the Seminole began to separate from the Creek and move south to Florida in the early 1700s, the Spanish had established a few settlements, including Saint Augustine in northeastern Florida.

The Spanish showed little interest in interacting or trading with the Seminole. The Indians retained their ties with British traders in Georgia and the Carolinas. At times, the Seminole attacked Spanish settlements. The Seminole chief Cowkeeper bragged that he had killed 86 Spaniards.

The Seminole were not the only newcomers to Florida in the early 1700s. Spain had outlawed slavery in Florida in 1693, making it a refuge for escaped slaves from farther north. Many settled with the Seminole. At times, the Seminole captured or bought slaves, but they had little need for slave labor. Instead, they allowed the slaves to set up their own communities nearby. The slaves paid the Seminole a small **TRIBUTE** from their harvest each year. In return, the Indians protected them from recapture by white slave hunters.

As he searched for gold and silver, Hernando de Soto stole food and kidnapped and enslaved American Indians.

Most of these slaves, who became known as Black Seminole, followed a lifestyle similar to that of the Seminole. According to one observer, the slaves "dress and live pretty much like the Indians, … they plant in common, and farm an Indian field apart, which they attend together." The Black Seminole fought alongside the Seminole Indians in battle as well. Many Black Seminole spoke English, Spanish, and Muskogee, so they often served as translators and advisers to Seminole chiefs.

In 1763, control of Florida passed from Spain to Britain. British traders set up posts throughout Florida. In return for deerskins and cattle hides, the British provided the Seminole with manufactured goods such as guns, tools, and cloth. While the Spanish had largely ignored the Seminole, the British established treaties to regulate the Indians. In 1765, several Lower Creek and Seminole chiefs attended a peace conference. There, British East Florida governor James Grant told them, "You are apprehensive and have been told that the white people are desirous of getting possession of your hunting grounds. Your fears are ill-founded for I am ordered by the Great King not to take any lands which are of use to you even if you should agree to give them up." He further told them that it would be to their benefit to live close to their "brothers the English," who could supply them with "clothes to cover you, your wives, and children, with guns, powder, and balls for your hunting, and with a number of other things which you cannot make for yourselves though you cannot exist without them."

The conference resulted in the signing of the Treaty of Picolata. The Creek and Seminole agreed to give up 2 million acres (809,371

Being Seminole

⭒⟶ **AGAINST EDUCATION** ⟵⭒ *For many years, the Seminole resisted the white education system. They believed, as one elder said, "As soon as an Indian learns to read and write, he learns to lie." Additionally, a Seminole council said, "If you teach our children the knowledge of the white people, they will cease to be Indians." Despite such objections, schools were eventually established on the reservations. The first Seminole graduated from high school in 1945. By the 1980s, many Seminole achieved a college education.*

ha) of land in return for British goods such as guns, blankets, and kettles. Creek and Seminole leaders emphasized that they under- stood the value of what they were giving up: "You will consider that the presents which are now to be given us may last for a year but will afterwards not [last] and [will] become of no value, but the land which we now give will last forever."

With friendly relations between the Seminole and the British settlers, most Seminole remained loyal to Britain during the **AMERICAN REVOLUTION**. The war had little direct effect on Florida, which remained a loyal British colony, but some Seminole took part in British raids across the Georgia border. They also helped defend Saint Augustine from attack.

Through the Treaty of Paris that ended the American Revolution, Florida passed back into Spanish control in 1783. Although relations between the Spanish and the Seminole were largely peaceful, the Indians began to come into conflict with Americans living across the Florida border in Georgia. Cattle and horse raiding became common on both sides. In addition, settlers began to take over Seminole hunting and cattle grazing grounds. The U.S. turned its eye toward seizing control of Florida.

TOURIST ATTRACTION *In the early 1900s, some Seminole lived in exhibition villages. For an admission fee, tourists could visit these villages and get a firsthand view of Seminole life. The Seminole who lived in the villages sold souvenirs, patchwork clothing, baskets, and dolls. Men wrestled alligators as a further attraction. In some exhibition villages, the Seminole staged weddings featuring the same bride and groom again and again. The Seminole families who lived in the villages received $6 a week, plus food, from the white businessmen who ran the ventures.*

In 1811, the U.S. put together a small force, known as the Patriot Army, to invade and take over Florida. The Patriot Army attempted to recruit the Seminole and their black allies to fight for the Americans. Both groups refused. Instead, they launched a fierce defense, which helped drive the Patriot Army out of Florida.

But the Americans didn't stay out of Florida long. In late 1817, General **ANDREW JACKSON** led 2,000 soldiers into Florida, under the guise of recapturing runaway slaves. In what became known as the First Seminole War, Jackson and his troops burned Seminole villages and fields. This forced the Indians and the Black Seminole to flee farther south. The troops also seized Spanish towns. As a result of the war, Spain had to give up Florida, which passed into U.S. control in 1821.

Within 2 years, the U.S. had signed its first treaty with the 5,000 Seminole who lived in Florida. Through the Treaty of Moultrie Creek, the Seminole agreed to give up 24 million acres (9.7 million ha) of land in return for a reservation in central Florida. But the location chosen for the reservation proved poor for farming. A drought in 1825 led to widespread starvation among the Seminole. To obtain food, some began to steal cattle from

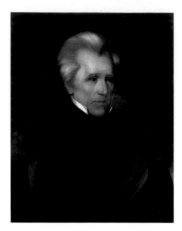

nearby settlers. Florida's government passed a law stating that any Seminole found off the reservation would be whipped 39 times on the bare back.

Despite the hardships they experienced in Florida, the Seminole considered it their homeland. When the U.S. government passed the Indian Removal Act in 1830, with the intention of moving Indians from the eastern U.S. to Indian Territory, most Seminole resisted. Young Seminole warrior Osceola led the resistance. He told his people, "We must not leave our homes and lands. If any of our people want to go west, we won't let them; and I tell them they are our enemies."

Despite such sentiments, several Seminole leaders signed the 1832 Treaty of Payne's Landing. The treaty stipulated that the Seminole would move to Indian Territory only if they could find suitable land there. In 1833, a group of seven Seminole men traveled to Indian Territory. There they were forced to sign a treaty stating that the land was acceptable, despite their protests that they had no authority to do so. Seminole leader Jumper later described what he thought he was signing: "The agents of the United States made us sign our hands to a paper, which you say signified our consent to remove; but we considered we did no more than say we liked the land, and when we returned, the [Seminole] nation would decide." Despite Jumper's protests, the U.S. government considered the treaty binding. The Seminole were expected to leave Florida by January 1, 1836.

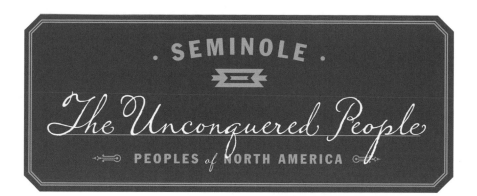

Although about 10 percent of the Seminole left voluntarily, the majority of the people refused to leave Florida. As American forces flooded into the area to forcibly remove them, the Seminole prepared for war. In December 1835, Seminole warriors attacked a **MILITIA** unit, ambushed U.S. soldiers, and killed an **INDIAN AGENT**. This was the start of the Second Seminole War. Osceola sent word to U.S. commanders: "You have guns, and so have we. You have powder and lead, and so have we. Your men will fight and so will ours, till the last drop of Seminole's blood has moistened the dust of his hunting ground."

For the next 7 years, a force of 800 Seminole warriors faced off against 5,000 U.S. soldiers and militia. Led by tacticians such as Osceola and **ARPEIKA**, the Seminole retreated deeper into the swamps of southern Florida. Here, they had an advantage, as the terrain was unfamiliar to the soldiers, who had to trudge through miles of marshy grasslands to reach them. Seeking cover on hammocks, the Seminole relied largely on guerrilla tactics to strike blows against their enemies before disappearing again. Meanwhile, soldiers destroyed Seminole homes and crops wherever they found them, leaving the Indians in need of food. In addition, the U.S. soldiers had better access

ARTIST GEORGE CATLIN TRAVELED TO FORT MOULTRIE, WHERE OSCEOLA WAS IMPRISONED, TO PAINT THE SEMINOLE LEADER'S PORTRAIT.

to gunpowder. Seminole losses began to mount.

In 1837, with his forces severely depleted, Osceola agreed to take part in peace talks. He and 80 Seminole came into an American camp under a white flag. Rather than negotiating, however, U.S. military commander Thomas Jesup seized the opportunity to imprison Osceola. The Seminole leader died three months later of illness.

FAMILIARITY WITH FLORIDA'S TERRAIN ENABLED THE SEMINOLE TO EVADE U.S. MILITARY FORCES.

Despite Osceola's capture, many Seminole continued to resist. But by 1841, about three-quarters of the Seminole in Florida had been captured or forced to surrender and sent to Indian Territory. In 1842, with only 500 Seminole remaining in Florida, the U.S. called off hostilities, and the army withdrew. All told, the Second Seminole War had cost the U.S. government more than $30 million and the lives of at least 1,500 soldiers. Hundreds of Seminole are believed to have died as well.

After the fighting ended, the Seminole were left in peace for a time on a Florida reservation. But the government continued to pressure them to leave for Indian Territory, offering large sums of money to any who agreed to go. In 1849, tensions mounted when a group of five Seminole men attacked white settlers. Although the Seminole on the reservation captured these renegades and turned them over to the U.S. government, the remaining Seminole were ordered to leave Florida. Seminole chief Assinwar expressed his anger at the order: "When you ask us to remove, I feel as though you had killed me, too. I will not go, nor will our people." Despite Seminole assurances that there would be no more trouble, U.S. forces moved onto the Seminole reservation. In response, the

BETTY MAE JUMPER ⟿ *Born in 1923, Betty Mae Jumper showed an early interest in education, sparked by her enjoyment of a comic book. She attended boarding school in North Carolina and received her high school diploma in 1945. She then studied nursing at Kiowa Indian Hospital in Oklahoma. Afterward, she returned to Florida, where she was named to the tribal council in 1957. Ten years later, she became the first female Seminole chief. She eventually served as director of a Seminole newspaper and also became a renowned Seminole storyteller.*

Seminole again fled into the swamps.

The Third Seminole War began in 1855 when a Seminole band under **BILLY BOWLEGS** attacked an army patrol that had destroyed their fields and camp. Nearly 1,500 U.S. soldiers and militia moved into Florida. Using flat-bottomed boats, they pursued the Seminole through the swamps for three years. Finally, in March 1858, Billy Bowlegs and his band agreed to move to Indian Territory, along with several other Seminole. Fewer than 200 Seminole remained in Florida, and the government declared the war over. A peace treaty was never signed, leading many Seminole to call themselves the "Unconquered People."

The 4,000 Seminole who had been relocated to Indian Territory worked to build a new life there. Although the government at first forced them to settle within the Creek nation, in 1855, the Seminole were allowed to form their own nation. They followed a lifestyle similar to what they had known in Florida, raising crops and grazing livestock, as well as hunting, fishing, and gathering. In 1906, Seminole lands, like those of other peoples in Indian Territory, faced **ALLOTMENT**. Each tribal member received a small tract of land. Any land remaining in the reservation after allotment was opened up for white settlement.

Meanwhile, the few Seminole who remained in Florida stayed hidden in the swamps. They avoided contact with white settlers for two decades. In the 1890s, the government began to purchase lands for the Florida Seminole, eventually establishing three reservations. At first, the Seminole refused to go near the reservations, but in the 1930s, many moved onto reservation lands to obtain food, healthcare, and other needed services.

In 1957, the Seminole Tribe of Florida was officially recognized. Some Seminole continued to live off the reservation. In 1962, many of these Seminole broke off to form the Miccosukee Tribe of

BILLY BOWLEGS (FARTHEST RIGHT), 38 WARRIORS, AND 85 WOMEN AND CHILDREN TRAVELED BY BOAT TO INDIAN TERRITORY.

Indians. Other Seminole, known as Traditional Seminole, refused to join either the Seminole Tribe or the Miccosukee but instead remained independent. Traditional Seminole opposed any government interference in their lives. "The white man ... does not try to know and respect our ways of life," said Traditional Seminole Jimmy Wilson. "He tries to make us one of his."

In the 1970s, the Seminole opened smoke shops to sell tax-free cigarettes. They also opened the first high-stakes bingo halls in North America. Over time, they added restaurants, hotels, and other tourist ventures. Such activities brought in millions of dollars for healthcare, law enforcement, and schools on the Seminole and Miccosukee reservations in Florida.

Today, about 27,000 people of Seminole descent live in the U.S. The majority live in Oklahoma, where many work in agriculture, oil, or construction. In Florida, many Seminole live on reservations at the edge of the Everglades. Some Miccosukee and

EVERGLADES RESTORATION *According to the Seminole Tribe of Florida, "the Tribe's identity is so closely linked to the land that Tribal members believe that if the land dies, so will the Tribe." Over the years, canals, dams, and pollution have affected the waters of the Everglades. As a result, the Seminole have launched the Seminole Everglades Restoration Initiative. This $65-million plan is designed to improve water quality in the Everglades by restoring water flow to drained areas, enhancing flood controls, and removing pollutants.*

Traditional Seminole continue to live in the swamps. Some live in chickees, while others, especially those on the reservations, live in structures of concrete block. Rather than dugout canoes, motorboats and airboats are used to maneuver through the swamps.

Despite these changes, some aspects of traditional Seminole culture remain strong. Many communities in both Florida and Oklahoma continue to celebrate the Green Corn Dance every year. Some tribal elders travel to schools to share their culture and music. Efforts have been made to preserve and pass on both the Muskogee and Mikasuki languages as well. In addition, tribal funds from gaming and other ventures have been used to set up cultural museums and festivals. As author James Covington points out, "It will be the young Seminoles whose choices decide the future of the tribe.... Of all the tribes in the United States, the Seminoles of Florida have been the most reluctant to adjust themselves to the white world." The Seminole people have experienced many changes, from their early days as part of the Creek Confederacy to their move into Florida and their fierce wars against the U.S. military. Through them all, the Seminole have fought hard to retain their culture and traditions as the Unconquered People.

SEMINOLE HOMELANDS IN SOUTHERN FLORIDA ARE HOME TO SOME OF THE LARGEST MANGROVE SWAMPS IN THE WORLD.

Around the evening campfire, Seminole children listened as elders told stories. According to Seminole storyteller Betty Mae Jumper, most of the stories were about "a time when the world was very young. A time when animals talked and walked on two feet." The stories told of mischievous creatures, gods, and how the world came to be. Some stories also taught important lessons. In this story, a hunter learns the importance of following his people's laws.

Long ago, two hunters lived at the edge of the Everglades. They spent their days hunting deer, birds, and turtles to feed their people. One day, the hunters made their way to Big Lake. When they arrived, they saw many animals all around the lake. They set up camp and went to sleep for the night.

The next day, they set out to hunt early in the morning. The hunters killed a large deer and spent the rest of the day cleaning it and smoking the meat. They were excited to have already found such success.

But when the men woke up the next day, it was raining. They had to stay in the camp all day. Once the rain finally stopped, one of the men went for a walk. When he returned, he brought with him two big bass. The second man asked where he had gotten them. He knew the first man had not carried any fishing equipment with him on his walk.

The first man said that he had found the fish jumping on the ground and picked them up. He was sure they must have fallen from the sky with the rain.

The second man told the first man to put the fish in the lake because he couldn't be sure where they had come from. But the man refused. He cleaned and cooked the fish and ate them.

Then the hunters went to sleep. But the man who had eaten the fish called out in the middle of the night. His friend came over to see what was wrong. The first man was turning into a snake. His legs had already disappeared and become a snake's tail. The snake man asked his friend to bring his family to him at the next full moon.

When the snake man's family arrived, his children were afraid of him. He had become a snake longer than a canoe. But the snake promised not to hurt them. He said he had something important to say, and after that, he would never be able to talk again. The snake told his family that he knew eating the fish he had found was against his people's laws but that he had done it anyway. He said becoming a snake was his punishment for doing wrong. Then he told his family to forget about him and to never come back because he wouldn't remember them and might hurt them. He swam out to the middle of the lake and, with one last wave of his tail, was gone.

ALLOTMENT
a system by which a portion of land was
set aside for an individual; many American
Indians were forced to take allotments
from tribal lands, with any remaining lands
going to the U.S. government

AMERICAN REVOLUTION
(1775–83) the war in which 13 British
colonies in North America fought Britain
for independence

ANDREW JACKSON
(1767–1845) army general who fought
many successful battles against Indian
tribes and in 1829 became the country's
seventh president; he signed the Indian
Removal Act, which relocated Indians to
lands west of the Mississippi River

ANTHROPOLOGISTS
people who study the physical traits,
cultures, and relationships of different
peoples

ARPEIKA
(c. 1765–1860) also known as Sam Jones;
Seminole medicine man who led resistance
to removal and was never captured; by
the end of hostilities, he was nearly 100
years old and remained in Florida with his
small band

BILLY BOWLEGS
(1810–59) also known as Holata Mikko;
Seminole chief who led resistance efforts
during the Third Seminole War but was
forced to relocate to Indian Territory
in 1858

CONFEDERACY
a group of nations or states that join
together for a specific purpose

GUERRILLA
having to do with fighting tactics that
involve undercover movements and
surprise attacks, usually carried out by a
small, independent group of fighters

INDIAN AGENT
someone assigned to deal with specific
Indian tribes on the government's behalf

INDIGENOUS
native to a specific place

MILITIA
an army made up of citizens instead of
professional soldiers

OSCEOLA
(1804–38) Seminole leader who led the
resistance to removal of the Seminole
from Florida to Indian Territory; he was
captured after coming to a peace talk under
a white flag

SHAMAN
a spiritual leader often believed to have
healing and other powers

THATCHED
covered with straw, reeds, or other plant
materials

TRIBUTE
payment made by one nation to another to
show submission or ensure protection

Calloway, Colin G. *The American Revolution in Indian Country: Crisis and Diversity in Native American Communities.* Cambridge: Cambridge University Press, 1995.

Covington, James W. *The Seminoles of Florida.* Gainesville: University Press of Florida, 1993.

Fairbanks, Charles H. *The Florida Seminole People.* Eds. Henry F. Dobyns and John I. Griffin. Phoenix: Indian Tribal Series, 1973.

Fogelson, Raymond D., ed. *Southeast.* Vol. 14 of *Handbook of North American Indians.* Ed. William C. Sturtevant. Washington, D.C.: Smithsonian, 2004.

Hatch, Thom. *Osceola and the Great Seminole War: A Struggle for Justice and Freedom.* New York: St. Martin's Press, 2012.

Page, Jake. *In the Hands of the Great Spirit: The 20,000-Year History of American Indians.* New York: Free Press, 2003.

Perdue, Theda, and Michael D. Green. *The Columbia Guide to American Indians of the Southeast.* New York: Columbia University Press, 2001.

Wickman, Patricia R. *Osceola's Legacy.* Tuscaloosa: University of Alabama Press, 1991.

⊷⇒ READ MORE ⇐⊶

Collinson, Clare, ed. *Peoples of the East, Southeast, and Plains.* Redding, Conn.: Brown Bear Books, 2009.

Girod, Christina M. *Native Americans of the Southeast.* San Diego: Lucent Books, 2001.

⊷⇒ WEBSITES ⇐⊶

AH-TAH-THI-KI MUSEUM
http://www.ahtahthiki.com/
Learn more about Seminole history and culture through this museum located on the Big Cypress Seminole Indian Reservation.

SEMINOLE TRIBE OF FLORIDA
http://www.semtribe.com/
Check out the official site of the Seminole Tribe of Florida to learn more about the Seminole way of life.